Original title:
Woodland Wisdom

Copyright © 2025 Creative Arts Management OÜ
All rights reserved.

Author: Evan Hawthorne
ISBN HARDBACK: 978-1-80567-202-9
ISBN PAPERBACK: 978-1-80567-501-3

Beneath the Birch

Under the birch, where squirrels play,
I asked a raccoon, 'What's the way?'
He scratched his head, gave me a joke,
Said, 'Just follow the trail where the mushrooms poke.'

A deer nearby just rolled his eyes,
Whispered to me, 'They're all such lies!'
But with a wink, she pranced away,
As if she'd heard the best wordplay.

Echoes in the Underbrush

In the brush, a chorus sings,
Frogs in tuxedos do their flings.
The owl hoots out a funny tale,
While crickets chirp a comic scale.

A fox in glasses reads the news,
Said, 'What's all this fuss about shoes?'
The rabbits hop with laughter loud,
While trees applaud, they are so proud.

Flight of the Feathered Sage

A wise old bird perched on a branch,
Said, 'To be wise, you must take a chance.'
He flapped his wings, to my surprise,
Declared, 'I'm smarter than all those flies!'

With ruffled feathers, he cracked a joke,
Spilled the secrets that bugs awoke.
His wisdom flew on every breeze,
As down below, we laughed with ease.

The Dappled Path

On the dappled path, I found a hat,
A sign it was owned by a clever cat.
Running in circles, he told me a tale,
Of fish who fly and cows that sail.

We followed a trail of taffy and sweets,
Till we stumbled on some dancing feet.
The ground shook with laughter all around,
On that path where joy was found.

Resilient Rhythms

In the trees a squirrel prances,
Chasing dreams in wild glances.
Falling acorns, what a treat!
It's a dance for tiny feet.

Mushrooms giggle in the shade,
While the rabbits play charade.
With every hop and twist they make,
They surely raise the forest quake.

The wise old owl rolls his eyes,
As raccoons plot their big surprise.
Stealing snacks like it's a game,
In this dance, they seek the fame.

But when it rains, they jump in puddles,
Splashing joy, shaking off cuddles.
Every drop brings laughter's tune,
In their hearts, they dance till noon.

The Fern's Folio

In the glen, the ferns convene,
Chit-chat grows, a leafy scene.
"Who wore best?" they giggle low,
Peeking past the fallen snow.

A hedgehog dons a dapper hat,
Twirling round with bits of chat.
"Who needs style?" the wild things roar,
To dance like this is quite the score!

The wise old badger shakes his head,
"Ladies first!" he gently said.
But mice in boots just can't resist,
And twirl and leap, they can't desist.

So let the laughter fill the air,
With frolics light as breezes fair.
In leafy realms where fun prevails,
The fern folk spin their playful tales.

Moonlit Paths of the Wild

When the moonlight paints the trees,
The raccoons dance with such great ease.
Owls hoot jokes from their high perch,
While fireflies waltz in a glowing search.

The shadows giggle, playfully sneaky,
As squirrels debate who's the most cheeky.
With mischief abound, the night's alive,
Nature's whispers, where laughter thrives.

The Song of the Singing Stream

The stream gurgles tunes of delight,
"Hey, fish! Join the dance tonight!"
With splashes from frogs that leap in joy,
Each ripple a laugh, a musical ploy.

The rocks hum along with a chipper beat,
While tadpoles twirl on their little feet.
"Hey there, snail, can you keep pace?
Join our party in this happy place!"

Guardians of the Green Realm

The trees don capes, with leaves of green,
In their branches, antics can be seen.
Squirrels recruit for a log-rolling team,
While wise old owls concoct a dream.

The hedgehogs guard with bristle and cheer,
Whispering secrets for all who hear.
"Quick, hide!" they cry at the fox's prance,
"Join us for a woodland dance!"

Messages Carried by the Wind

The wind delivers funny tales,
Of chipmunks swiping all the snails.
It rustles leaves with a giggling sound,
As whispers of humor swirl around.

"Hey, let's prank the sleeping bear!
Or shall we scatter seeds in the air?"
On gusts of laughter the jokes take flight,
Nature's jesters, through day and night.

Murmurs of the Mossy Path

In the woods where the mushrooms chat,
A squirrel borrowed a fancy hat.
He stumbled and tumbled down the hill,
Whispering secrets that gave us a thrill.

The old owl hooted a riddle or two,
While rabbits played hopscotch as a crew.
The trees giggled as the breeze swayed,
Trading tall tales in a leafy parade.

Dancing with Dappled Light

Beneath branches that shimmer and flash,
A deer pranced by in a giant splash.
With a boogie and jig, the fawns take flight,
In a dance-off against the fading light.

The sunbeams chuckle upon the ground,
As ladybugs waltz, round and round.
The butterflies twirl in colorful grace,
While worms groove on, with the slowest pace.

Nature's Silent Counsel

A wise old tree leaned in to say,
'Life's a picnic, on a sun-kissed day.'
With branches waving, it shared a joke,
While a nearby boulder began to poke.

The brook's water snickered with delight,
As frogs in tuxedos leaped left and right.
'Take it easy, the forest will play,
Just avoid those ants with a chip on their fray!'

Footprints on Ferns

Tiny feet ventured where fairies dwell,
Walking softly, casting off a spell.
They tripped over roots, giggles in air,
Kissing each fern with a playful flair.

A raccoon joined in with a clumsy jig,
His friends laughed hard, 'He's really a big!'
As mud splattered wide, and laughter rang,
The ferns whispered secrets, in the daylight's fang.

The Bramble's Secret

In thickets thick, the brambles chuckle,
They tickle toes and cause a shuffle.
A squirrel laughs, steals a nut so grand,
But trips and falls—oh, on his face he lands!

The hedgehog rolls, with a spiky grin,
A dance of joy as the day begins.
They share their snacks, the berries red,
While rabbits contemplate what's next ahead.

The snap of twigs is laughter loud,
As foxes frolic, feeling proud.
But watch your back, the birds might sing,
When you're caught in a joke—a silly fling!

So wander through, let joy ignite,
In bramble realms where laughter's bright.
Embrace the fun, and don't be shy,
For nature's secrets draw a smile nigh!

The Whispering Willows

Beneath the willows, shadows sway,
They gossip softly, night and day.
A breeze carries tales of silly things,
Of owls in glasses and squirrel kings.

The frogs in chorus, so off-key,
Croak about dreams of honey tea.
While crickets hold their music tight,
In a battle with fireflies to shine the bright.

"Who stole my worm?" a worm claims loud,
"Not me," says the snail, creeping proud.
And bees trade jokes about nectar spills,
As laughter tumbles down the hills.

So join the choir, the willow's call,
With a chuckle, joy can't help but sprawl.
In every whisper, fun takes flight,
Among the trees, heartwarming delight!

Dreams of the Deserted Grove

In a grove where shadows play,
The trees share dreams in a funny way.
"Imagine if we grew legs to prance!"
Laughed the oak, starting a tree dance!

An elder bush rolled its leafy eyes,
"And what if we wore fancy ties?"
The crows cawed back, "What a sight to see,
A dapper bunch of trees—oh, whee!"

Said the lilac with a giggly air,
"I'd strut around without a care!"
Then a rustle—who could it be?
The wild mushrooms joined in, so carefree!

Amidst the chuckles and leafy cheer,
The grove is a stage, the fun is clear.
They dream together, so bizarre and bold,
In a world where laughter never gets old!

Moonlit Murmurs

At dusk, the moon begins to rise,
The forest laughs, beneath the skies.
"Let's play hide and seek," the shadows say,
"Who can hide from the moon today?"

The raccoons giggle, so full of schemes,
Under stars, they chase their dreams.
While moles plan mischief, all in jest,
"Let's tickle the badger, he's the best!"

Then comes a thud—oh what a sound!
The rabbits leap from the underground.
"Did you hear that?" whispers the hare,
"Was it a prank, or a monster there?"

But it's only the grass that bends and sways,
Joining the fun in this moonlit haze.
Among the chuckles, the world feels bright,
In this whispering night, laughter takes flight!

Guardians of the Green

In the grove where acorns clatter,
Squirrels gossip, oh, what's the matter?
A rabbit spills tea on a mushroom hat,
While a wise old turtle giggles, 'Look at that!'

The hedgehog strums on strings made from grass,
A beat so silly, you'll laugh and pass.
With every twist and every turn,
Nature's jesters have tales to churn.

Shadows in the Thicket

In the shadows, a frog tells a joke,
'Why did the chicken?'—it's a total poke!
A fox in a tie, he's a sight to see,
Sipping on tea with a bumbling bee.

'You're looking sharp, my spiky friend!'
Said the owl, laughing till it had to bend.
A dance-off starts with leaves in flight,
While the raccoons tumble, oh what a sight!

The Owl's Ancient Tale

An owl perched high with spectacles grand,
   Shares a story in a hooting band.
  'Once there was a nut that rolled away,
It caused quite the ruckus, such a funny fray!'

With squirrels in capes and mice in a car,
  On a quest to find their lost nut star.
   But every time they took a peek,
The nut just giggled, 'Can't catch me, meat!'

Roots that Bind

Underneath the roots, a party's arranged,
A beetle DJ has the crowd changed.
'This beat's un-bug-lievable!' they all cheer,
As fireflies twinkle, spreading good cheer.

For every twist and every turn tight,
The critters come out in the soft moonlight.
And as the sun rises, hear them proclaim,
'Let's do it again! In nature's name!'

Beneath the Boughs of Time

Beneath the branches, squirrels debate,
Why acorns always seem to be late.
The owls hoot secrets, wise and sly,
While nutty thoughts drift up to the sky.

The rabbits gossip about their grand plans,
While badgers join in with their funky dance.
The mossy carpet tells tales untold,
Of mushroom parties that never grow old.

Frogs leap in rhythm, croaking their tunes,
As crickets join in beneath glowing moons.
Each thumping foot falls in perfect beat,
With nature's laughter echoing sweet.

So if you wander by these trees so grand,
Join in the fun and lend them a hand.
For beneath the boughs, with a wink and a grin,
Lies a world of laughter just waiting to spin.

The Heartbeat of Trees

In the heart of the forest, the trees take a pulse,
Tick-tocking to rhythms that make them convulse.
The pinecones chuckle as breezes roll by,
While vines intertwine, gossipy and spry.

The raccoons are plotting a comedic heist,
For snacks they declare are too fun to be spliced.
With branches like arms, they reach out for treats,
Telling tall tales of their picturesque feats.

A log's belly laughs as a beetle slips by,
Wobbling and tumbling, oh my, oh my!
Mice share their cheese jokes that just never end,
While hedgehogs and swans agree, "Let's pretend!"

So next time you wander through this lively scene,
Join in the fun, be silly, be keen.
For the trees hold a rhythm that's happy and free,
With laughter embedded in their grand symphony.

Tales Woven in Twigs

There's gossip in branches, spun from some twigs,
Of fanciful creatures who dance like they're pigs.
The owls are the judges, perched high on their thrones,
While hedgehogs serve tea in their tiny, sly tones.

A raucous array of beetles unite,
To put on a play 'neath the glow of moonlight.
With acorn hats and a knack for the jest,
They shimmer in shadows, they're simply the best.

Bunnies are laughing, they leap with delight,
As fireflies flicker, oh what a sight!
They gleefully prance on the path made of ferns,
When a squirrel shouts "Wait!" for the popcorn that churns.

So if ever you glimpse a twiggy parade,
Know it's nature's humor, beautifully made.
Join in their stories, their giggles, their cheer,
For the forest is full of laughter, oh dear!

Shadows of the Elder Oak

Under the oak, where shadows delight,
The squirrels are scheming their next little flight.
With acorn hats on and a mischievous smirk,
They plan little raves that make the leaves twerk.

Chipper and chipmunks are breaking the rules,
Dancing in circles and acting like fools.
Their rhymes grow louder, jubilant and clear,
While the crows caw loudly, joining the cheer.

A rabbit arrives, with a joke on the side,
"Why did the tree blush? It was stumped by its pride!"
As giggles erupt from the undergrowth spry,
A chorus of laughter swells up to the sky.

So if you find you need a good grinning,
Seek out the oak where the fun's ever spinning.
In nature's embrace, let the laughter flow,
For the shadows hold secrets that only they know.

Fragments of Fern Fronds

In the forest, ferns do dance,
Whispering secrets, given a chance.
They giggle at squirrels, chubby and bold,
Bragging of acorns, tasty and gold.

Mossy hats for the mushy feet,
A snail's slow race, not so elite.
Frogs croak jokes on a lily pad,
While dragonflies chuckle, oh so glad.

The trees stand tall, wise and spry,
Teaching the flowers how to fly.
"Try not to trip on your blooms," they say,
As bees roll by, buzzing in play.

Take a step in the leafy maze,
Join in the laughter, savor the days.
Nature's giggles, it's clear to see,
In every fracture of leaf and tree.

A Tapestry of Twigs

Twigs weave tales in a knotted dance,
Of a raccoon's love for a bright green pants.
They gossip of rabbits, silly and spry,
Who think they can dance but just hop by.

Branches with stories of far-off lands,
From owls who hoot with their wise old hands.
"Are we here for fun, or just for the news?"
The woodpecker giggles, "Whatever you choose!"

Bark covered tales of the wind's wild tricks,
Chasing acorns and hiding their picks.
When asked for advice, the leaves just sway,
"Grab your basket, come dance, come play!"

A patchwork of laughter stitched with a breeze,
All creatures join in: it's sure to please.
Nature's jesters, so lively, so spry,
A tapestry formed 'neath the brightening sky.

When the Sun Speaks Softly

When sunlight whispers through the trees,
It tickles the branches, like a tease.
"Hey, sprightly buds, wake up with glee,
Let's play a game, just you and me!"

The shadows stretch and dance with delight,
Crickets tell stories that spark into light.
Mushrooms giggle at the passing ants,
While bees sing songs of their sunny plans.

As petals stretch wide, they share a grin,
Hiding their dreams since the day they began.
"Let's play hopscotch on that sunbeam there,
Or build a tall tower from this sweet air!"

When the sun speaks soft, nature plays loud,
Embracing the fun in the bustling crowd.
Every rustle and giggle blends into one,
In the warm embrace of a day just begun.

Buoyant Breezes of Belief

Breezes come whistling, light and spry,
Spreading the joy as they flip on by.
"Float with us, leaves, let's twirl and spin,
Who knew the forest had such a grin?"

The dandelions beam, puffing with pride,
As they blow wishes on the soft tide.
"Catch me if you can!" the butterflies tease,
While the wise old oak leans back with ease.

Laughter entwines with the rustling sound,
Every gust carries giggles around.
A brisk little breeze, how clever, how neat,
Plays hide and seek under each tree's seat.

So join in the frolic, believe in the fun,
Dance with the brambles, no need to run.
For in nature's embrace, we find our relief,
In the buoyant breezes of this wild belief.

Keeping Time with the Treetops

The trees all wear their rings with pride,
Counting years like a timekeeper's guide.
Squirrels chirp, they check their clocks,
"Now is the time for acorn stocks!"

Branches wave as they share tall tales,
Of lumberjack feats and autumn gales.
Each gust of wind, a gentle chime,
"Look out below, it's acorn time!"

The owls hoot with a wink so sly,
As the forest's gossip travels by.
"I heard it's spring, let's shed some leaves!"
"Oh no, not again, this forest grieves!"

So let's join in this leafy jest,
As nature plays its very best.
With laughter ringing through the trees,
We'll dance like branches in the breeze.

Lessons in Lichen

On rocks and trees, they stick and grow,
A colorful duo, putting on a show.
"Hey, did you hear? No need for soil!"
Lichen laughs, "We just love toil!"

They teach us patience, slow and steady,
"Why race the sun? You've got time, be ready!"
With a sprinkle of rain and a kiss of sun,
They thrive together, oh what fun!

Moss joins in with a velvet grin,
"Look at us, we're cousins of kin!
Let's share our secrets, the art of chill,
Life's a long climb, but we've got the skill!"

So next time you wander, pause for a peek,
At lichen's dance, so mild, yet sleek.
With humor woven in their thread,
They remind us to laugh, even just instead.

The Narrative of Nature

In the heart of the woods, each leaf does tell,
A story of seasons, of sunshine and swell.
"Once we danced in spring's bright light,"
Now we shuffle through autumn's fright!"

The rocks mutter tales of the weathered years,
"Through storms and calm, we've shed our fears.
Each crack a chapter, each crevice a page,
We've seen many critters, and they've acted their age!"

Fluffy clouds gather to gossip up high,
"Did you see that rabbit? It leapt to the sky!
With each little leap, he thinks he can fly,
But let's not forget, he's not a blue sky!"

Nature chuckles, weaving humor so fine,
Bringing laughter through vines, in each twist and twine.
So turn your ears to the rustling song,
And join in the fun, you can't go wrong!

Glimpses through the Glade

In the glade, where shadows play,
The critters gather to have their say.
"Did you see the deer's fumble today?
Tripped on her hooves, oh what a display!"

The hedgehogs chuckle, rolling with glee,
"Not as clumsy as that bee, hee-hee!"
They bump and nudge, in a circle of cheer,
Each story getting sillier, as friends draw near.

The sun peeks through, a mischievous ray,
"Watch your belly, let's all sway!"
One foolish fox tries to out-dance the sun,
But ends up tangled, oh wasn't that fun!

So let the glade be your stage tonight,
Where laughter echoes in pure delight.
With every rustle, each flutter and fling,
Nature's a jester, oh how she can sing!

Cradle of the Woodland Spirits

In a tree stump, a squirrel doth play,
Telling tales of acorns and hay.
His friends all laugh with glee and cheer,
For mischief awaits when nuts are near.

The owls are wise, with spectacles grand,
They vote on who's the best in the band.
A raccoon juggles berries with pride,
While the fox croons songs that he can't quite hide.

The flowers gossip about the sun,
"Isn't he charming? It's all in good fun!"
Yet the mushrooms shake heads in disdain,
"Someone's too bright; it's such a rain."

So laugh with the spirits, frolic and twist,
For if you don't laugh, you'll be sorely missed.
Join hands in the glade where silliness thrives,
And let the dance of the woodland come alive!

Secrets Told by the Rustling Reeds

In the marsh where the reeds sway and talk,
They tease the frogs who dance on their clock.
"Oh dear little critters, don't leap too high!
You'll soon find yourself in the mud awry!"

Grasshoppers chirp like jesters of old,
Sharing light tales that never get old.
"A dragonfly's hat? It's surely too grand!
It keeps flying off; isn't life unplanned?"

The turtles laugh slow, with their heads tucked in,
"They talk about fashion; where do we begin?"
Yet, wise as they seem, with shells they're secure,
In the world of fashion, they'll always endure.

So next time you stroll past the rustling green,
Listen closely for giggles that swirl and convene.
Even the wind adds its own little jest,
In the ballet of nature, we're all truly blessed!

In the Company of Ferns

Amongst the ferns where the shadows play,
A snail declared, "I'm leading the way!"
The others all chuckled, "Oh what a joke!
You'll reach the end when you start to soak!"

A hedgehog rolled in, spines all a-glow,
"I'm here for the party; I brought the show!"
The ferns all swayed, "We love a good dance!
But mud on our fronds? It'll ruin our chance!"

A rabbit hopped in with a flourish to boast,
"I can jump higher than anyone's toast!"
But a wise old tortoise just winked and said,
"Jumping is great, but have you tried bread?"

So gather your friends in the shadowy glen,
Where laughter's the dress code for critters and men.
In the company of ferns, let the fun unfurl,
For every good joke makes a bright, happy world!

Omens in the Underbrush

Below the bushes, the critters convene,
With tales of omens both strange and obscene.
"A leaf that drops? It's a sign of a feast!
Time for a picnic, to say the least!"

A beetle intones in a voice oh-so low,
"Did you hear that? The wind has a flow.
If it whispers 'cheese,' you better beware;
For cheese in the woods leads to raccoons' lair!"

The rabbits all nod, so wise in their haste,
"We're masters of fortune, not one to waste.
A dash to the carrots is surely good luck,
Especially if there's time for a pluck!"

So watch for signs where the shadows entwine,
For wisdom is silly wrapped up in a vine.
In the underbrush, where the omens are bright,
Every giggle and snicker is pure delight!

Beneath the Foliage's Embrace

Under leaves of emerald hue,
Squirrels claim their acorn brew.
Mice break dance on forest floors,
While owls watch with gossiping roars.

The sun peeks through in playful rays,
To tickle fawns in silly ways.
Streams giggle as they rush along,
A symphony of nature's song.

Frogs recite their croaky prose,
While butterflies wear fancy clothes.
Blades of grass have secrets to share,
With whispers carried through the air.

In this realm of laughter bright,
The trees tell tales until the night.
Even shadows join the jest,
In the embrace of a leafy nest.

Silhouettes at Dusk

At dusk the trees begin to sway,
Their shadow puppets start to play.
The rabbits leap with clumsy grace,
As darkness brings a cheeky face.

The moon, a lantern in the sky,
Winks at the stars, oh my, oh my!
Crickets chirp a tune offbeat,
A dance of chaos, oh how sweet!

Foxes, dressed in coats of flair,
Prance about without a care.
They say the night has much to teach,
Like not to nibble on a peach!

Bats take flight in silly loops,
Chasing after moths like stoops.
Laughter echoes through the trees,
At dusk, all join this jokester spree.

The Spirit of the Silent Pines

In the pines, where stillness hums,
A chipmunk thumps and often drums.
Each cone a treasure, ripe for tricks,
As nature's laughter surely ticks.

The pines stand tall, with wisdom old,
Yet love to giggle, bold and bold.
They whisper tales of bears who dance,
And view the world through nutty prance.

Each needle shines like a mustache fine,
On artists critiquing the moonlit line.
A squirrel debates, "Which way to roam?"
As tree trunks laugh from their comfy home.

Moss greets passing feet with jokes,
As shadows tease and play like folks.
In the hush of evergreens so grand,
Even silence seems to understand.

Conversations with the Oldest Root

Beneath the boughs where whispers creep,
An ancient root begins to leap.
"Why do we plant ourselves so deep?"
"Because we dream in earthen sleep!"

A wiggly worm joins in the chat,
"Why fret for things that hide like a cat?"
The root replies with a chuckle and shake,
"Because my friend, it's fun to partake!"

The mushrooms giggle, as if in on the joke,
While leaves dance lightly, praising the poke.
"Do I smell pizza from the sky?"
"Not yet, dear root, just passin' by!"

With every breeze, a message clear,
Nature's humor brings us cheer.
In this lively grove, we all convene,
To share our laughter, so evergreen.

The Treetop Oracle

In the branches high, a squirrel prattles,
Chasing tales and shiny prattles.
"Why do humans wear such boots?"
"They're not for climbing, just for hoots!"

The owl spins wisdom in riddled night,
"Whose bright idea was to saunter in fright?"
The raccoons laugh with a flick of their tails,
"It's the shiny things that lead to our trails!"

The oracles chat, they giggle and tease,
"Can you tap dance on leaves in the breeze?"
With nuts in their cheeks, they plot and they plan,
"Who's the wisest? Obviously, the tan!"

And when dusk falls with a sleepy delight,
The treetops whisper stories through night.
So take off your shoes, come join for some fun,
In the realm of the trees, we're all number one!

The Stillness Speaks

When the quiet comes, the crickets conspire,
"Did you hear that? A shoe from the mire!"
The trees roll their eyes, they've seen it before,
"Another lost person, what's next in store?"

The deer on the path snickers with glee,
"I think they just tripped; was that really a bee?"
The shadows are chuckling from dusk till dawn,
As the lost wanderer sheepishly fawns.

With whispers of leaves and giggles in air,
"Who wears socks with sandals? How can they dare?"
The wind scoffs softly, a breeze full of sass,
"Maybe it's fashion... or just pure crass!"

Yet in this stillness, lessons are spun,
About the mishaps and laughter, lots of fun.
In nature's embrace, we can learn to play,
And let the stillness brighten our day!

Questions from the Quercus

Old Oak stands tall with a grin on his bark,
"Why do squirrels hoard acorns in the dark?"
With a wobble and bounce, he tries not to snicker,
"Maybe they're saving for winter's big snicker!"

A badger walks by, checking his watch,
"Do you think I'm late for my evening match?"
The Oak chuckles deep, leaves rustling away,
"Did you forget? You're never on display!"

The woodpecker taps with a rhythm so spry,
"What's with all the fuss? Let the forest fly high!"
The Oak rolls his eyes, and his branches he shakes,
"Sometimes they just need to lighten their fakes!"

And as day turns to night, the stars come in sight,
With laughter around, everything feels right.
From acorns to badgers, they all have their say,
In the grand scheme of trees, we are all here to play!

Fables of the Fern

In a patch of green, where the ferns love to sway,
 "Why do leaves rustle? Is it dance or a play?"
They chuckle and shimmy in sunshine so bright,
 "We're just stretching, getting ready for night!"

A beetle declares with a puffed-out chest,
 "What's the secret to feeling the best?"
The ferns giggle low, shivering with cheer,
"Just wear your own stripes with nothing to fear!"

An ant sneaks a peek, all busy and small,
 "Is there room for me in this laughter ball?"
"Of course! Come and join, we save you a place,
 It's fun with big smiles and plenty of space!"

As twilight approaches with fireflies' glow,
They twirl and they laugh, putting on quite a show.
In the world of green, the fables take flight,
 Reminding us all to embrace pure light!

Whispers of the Ancient Grove

In the twisty twigs, the squirrels conspire,
Chasing their tails, they never tire.
A wise old owl, with glasses askew,
Says, 'Don't take life so seriously, boo!'

The mushrooms gossip, so bold and spry,
'Have you heard the joke about the sly fly?'
They chuckle and giggle, under bright ferns,
While the sleepy hedgehog simply turns and yearns.

The trees throw shade, but they're just in jest,
'We only drop leaves when we're feeling blessed!'
Their branches sway, as if to say,
'Life is about dancing, come join our play!'

As bugs hold debates on who is the best,
A beetle declares, 'I've passed every test!'
But the butterfly flutters, with colors bright,
Saying, 'Real joy comes from taking flight!'

Secrets Beneath the Canopy

Beneath the leaves, where shadows twist,
A chipmunk plays, one paw clenched in a fist.
'What's the secret,' he squeaks with glee,
'Is it acorns or just maple tea?'

The badgers roll out their comedy routine,
With puns about mud, they're always obscene.
'Why do the worms play hide-and-seek?'
'Cause if they're found, they're in for a tweak!'

The forest floor is a giggle fest,
With ants sporting hats, in a funky dress.
They toil and they laugh, it's quite the scene,
In their bustling world, they're royalty keen.

Even the shadows have jokes up their sleeve,
'Why did the leaf decide to leave?'
It wanted adventure, to soar up high,
'Don't worry,' it said, 'I'll still wave goodbye!'

The Language of Leaves

In the rustling leaves, a language flows,
As the trees gossip, everybody knows.
'Tell me a secret,' the birch tree sighs,
'Was it you who painted the sunset skies?'

The cedar chuckles, 'Oh, that's an old tale,
But it was me who inspired the ship's sail!'
The pines whisper softly, but they can't keep still,
They shout, 'We're the stars of this leafy drill!'

A curious crow starts the day with a caw,
'Let's settle it now—who's the wisest of all?'
The leaves rustle back, with a nod and a sway,
'Every tree's clever in its own quirky way!'

So dance all around, as the branches sway,
In this leafy debate, come join and play.
Each crinkle and crumple, a joke on the breeze,
Bringing laughter and joy, hidden 'neath the trees.

Echoes of the Forest Floor

On the forest floor, where the giggles grow,
A critter parade puts on quite the show.
'Twinkle toes!' squeaks a mouse in delight,
As bouncy mushrooms spring into sight.

The fallen leaves form a crackling band,
Playing tunes only woodland creatures understand.
The snails keep time with their shells on parade,
While the nettles dance, uninvited but unafraid.

The acorns roll, telling stories of yore,
Of feasts and wild games, and daring galore.
A wise old tortoise grins at the fun,
'Life's not a race, just sit back and run!'

With echoes of laughter, the forest awakes,
A chorus of joy, from the tiniest stakes.
In every nook, there is mischief galore,
Just listen closely, hear the forest's roar!

Sparrow's Perspective

Up high on a branch, I spy a cat,
A furry little beast, quite round and fat.
He thinks he's a hunter, sleek and spry,
But I'm just a sparrow, watch me fly!

I chirp at the trees, they shake with glee,
They hear my jokes, they laugh with me.
The sun shines bright, like a grinning face,
Even the bushes join the merry chase!

My flock and I gather, share our tales,
Of epic worm hunts and windy gales.
We bestow silly names like Sir Wormington,
As we hop around, just having fun!

So if you see a feathered crew up there,
Know we're plotting mischief—if you dare!
With a chirp and a tweet, we'll brighten your day,
It's all in good spirit, come out and play!

The Echo Chamber of Earth

Deep in the woods, the echoes sing,
A chorus of critters, what joy they bring!
A squirrel squeaks out, a tune so strange,
The stuff of wild legends, absurd and deranged.

The rabbits all giggle at a bad pun,
While ants hold a meeting, plotting their run.
"I swear I heard that from a frog," they say,
As they bounce in their boots, hip-hop all the way!

The rocks start to rattle from laughter and sound,
As mushrooms all chuckle, springing from ground.
They hold onto secrets, many to share,
With roots in the soil that tickle the air!

In this echo chamber, nothing's quite right,
Truth gets a twist, from morning to night.
So listen closely, you might just find,
A giggle or snicker from nature, so kind!

Guardians of the Grove

Beneath the big trees, the guardians play,
With leafy hats and a lively display.
The wise old owl wears glasses so thick,
He looks quite ridiculous, that is his trick!

The raccoons hold council, they plot and they scheme,
Deciding which treasure to take from a dream.
"Shiny things first!" calls a sly little one,
While the others all ponder, "What's more fun?"

Meanwhile, the badger gives sage advice,
"Don't eat the berries, they've got quite a price!"
His wisdom is fruit, though it's often ignored,
As critters dive headfirst into tasty hoards.

With jokes and antics, they keep it light,
These guardians of laughter, heroes of night.
In a grove full of giggles, life is a treat,
Filled with whimsical moments that can't be beat!

The Celestial Canopy

Beneath a vast sky, the branches entwine,
A canopy dreams, quite lavish and fine.
With stars as the sprinkles on night's fluffy cake,
It's where light dances and silly dreams wake.

The moon whispers secrets to the crickets' song,
While fireflies flicker, bustling along.
"Hey, catch me if you can!" one shouts with glee,
As he twirls and twirls, a glow-filled spree!

The constellations giggle, playing their game,
Rearranging their spots, no two nights the same.
While the trees tell tales of the old, wise night,
Of the mischief and pranks that filled them with light.

So lie on the ground, gaze up at the spheres,
Let go of your worries, release all your fears.
In this celestial wonder, we'll laugh and we'll play,
In the arms of the night, where joy leads the way!

An Invitation from the Wild

Come join the frogs in their springtime show,
They dance on lily pads, as if to say hello!
The squirrels jest, with their acorn surprise,
While owls hoot jokes, under starry skies.

The trees play charades, their branches a mess,
While bushes gossip, causing quite a stress.
A raccoon in a top hat takes center stage,
Telling tall tales of a far-off age.

The grass tickles toes, a playful tease,
Breezes chuckle softly, as leaves start to wheeze.
Uninvited foxes play games of tag,
While badgers roll dice, and the snails just brag.

So heed this call, if you're up for some fun,
In the wild, laughter shines brighter than the sun!
Bring not your worries, just a grin and a snack,
For nature's giggles hold you, and never look back.

Hidden Chronicles of the Glade

In a secret nook where the shadows bask,
The trees share secrets, if you dare to ask.
Squirrels scribble tales in nutty scrawl,
While moles lend their ears, trusting one and all.

A fairy with glasses reads under the moon,
Reciting old fables in a comical tune.
The hedgehogs gather, sipping bramble tea,
Chortling loud tales of a blustery bee.

There's gossip of owls with very odd hats,
And who spooked the badgers while chasing their rats.
Every creature listens, wide-eyed with glee,
As secrets of the glade continue to be.

So stroll through the foliage, heed every sound,
For laughter is lurking, just waiting to be found!
The stories are silly, enchanting, and bright,
In this quirky glade, everything feels right.

The Pinecone Prophecy

Gather 'round, critters, the pinecones proclaim,
That wisdom flows freely, like a hilarious game.
The squirrels are wise, with their nutty advice,
"Don't trust a big mushroom, it may not be nice!"

The ferns wave a caution to beetles in flight,
"Watch out for the hawks with hilarious bites!"
While rabbits debate, with their floppy big ears,
On the best way to handle their flower fears.

The pines whisper tales of their needle-like fate,
"Don't get stuck in branches, or you could be late!"
As the wind stirs the laughter, as soft as a sigh,
"Your worries are funny, just let them all fly!"

So heed well, dear creatures, this quirky decree,
For wisdom is funny, if you just let it be!
A giggle awaits, in every tall tale,
Where pinecones predict with a whimsical wail.

Serpent of the Stream

A serpent with spectacles swims through the brook,
Reading fish gossip from a slippery book.
He chuckles at minnows, who tease and parade,
In a splashy ballet, they've got it made!

"Catch me if you can!" the splashes resound,
As frogs join the chorus, leaping around.
The dragonflies dart, with their shimmering grace,
As the serpent gives lessons in cool water space.

"Don't nibble the bait!" he warns with a wink,
"Or you might end up as someone's drink!"
The bubbles are giggling, the stones start to sway,
For life in the stream is a comical play.

With waves of laughter, the current flows bright,
As the serpent weaves tales in the soft morning light.
So dive in with joy, let your troubles take flight,
For the serpent invites you to join in the delight!

The Echo of Enduring Air

In the whispering breeze, a secret's told,
Trees giggle softly, as leaves unfold.
A squirrel throws acorns with playful glee,
Claiming the crown of the nutty decree.

The mushrooms all nod, they're wise and neat,
Holding their meetings under the seat.
When critters debate, it's quite a big fuss,
'Who's stealing my lunch?' says the curious bus.

Beneath the old oak, a rabbit takes notes,
While hedgehogs in suits discuss their fine coats.
They laugh at the clumsy, the snail in a race,
Winning by patience, a slow, steady pace.

So here in the air, where the laughter flows,
Nature's the teacher, as everyone knows.
So next time you wander, and hear them all cheer,
Remember the woodland's light-hearted sphere.

Treasures of the Timberland

A raccoon in goggles, so stylish and sleek,
Plans out a treasure hunt just for the week.
With a map made of bark and a compass of twigs,
He rallies his pals, two badgers and pigs.

They dig in the dirt, what a glorious sight!
Uncovering wild snacks from morning till night.
Carrots, and peanuts, and berries galore,
They feasted like kings, then went for some more.

A deer named Dinah, with elegance rare,
Joined in the fun, with a twirl and a flair.
Her hoofed dance puzzled the dogs with delight,
As they pranced and played till the fall of the night.

With treasures all gathered, they laughed and they sang,
In the heart of the woods where the merry bells rang.
So if you get lost, just follow the cheer,
There's treasure in laughter, forever held dear.

The Pondering Pine

There stood a tall pine, with branches galore,
He pondered the mysteries of life, to be sure.
With a wink and a nod, he'd share his wise thoughts,
On squirrels and nut-gathering, and all the free slots.

'Why chase the wind when the sun's so much fun?'
He'd chuckle each morning, a playful pun.
'Think of the bees and their sweet little dance,
They work hard, but watch how they twirl and prance.'

With needles for pencils, he scribbled away,
Jotting down thoughts on a long summer's day.
His friends gathered 'round, their curiosity piqued,
As he mused about life and the joy it leaked.

'Life's not just questions; it's laughter and cheer,
With a sprinkle of joy and a dash of good beer.'
So ponder, dear friends, let your thoughts lightly glide,
Embrace the refrain of the forest's joyride.

Myth of the Meadow

In the meadow so bright, where the daisies all tease,
A legend emerged under tall sunny trees.
They say if you sprinkle some pollen at noon,
A dance party starts with a song from the moon.

With rabbits in top hats and raccoons in disguise,
They shimmy and shake, oh what a surprise!
The butterflies flutter, adding to the cheer,
Chasing the rhythm, drawing everyone near.

The wise old owl, in the rafters above,
Brought down his wisdom, wrapped in a glove.
He'd wink to the fox, who wouldn't let slide,
The tales of the meadow and its jubilant pride.

So revel and laugh, if you hear them enthrall,
This myth of the meadow connects us with all.
For each little creature, with spirit so bright,
Craves fun in the sun, from morning till night.

A Conclave of Canopies

Underneath the leafy club,
The squirrels hold a scrappy hub.
They gossip over acorn stew,
While planning pranks for me and you.

With chestnut crowns and feathered caps,
They laugh and spin their nutty laps.
A council of the quirky tree,
With laughter ringing wild and free.

When autumn's chill begins to bite,
They stage a dance of sheer delight.
With twirling leaves as their grand stage,
Each squirrel shows off newfound rage.

They bounce and bound from trunk to branch,
In nature's zany, wiggly dance.
Oh, what a sight, that furry crew,
In whispers of the forest zoo!

Ties that Bind the Bark

Within the bark, the stories hide,
Of feisty beetles trying to ride.
A race across the twisted grain,
They giggle as they laugh in vain.

The slugs, they slither, slowly slide,
With secret meetings held inside.
They pen their tales in sticky trails,
While dreaming deep of leafy gales.

The woodpeckers join the fun,
In pitter-pat, they make their run.
Creating rhythms, drums they pound,
In operas of the trees, resound!

As roots entwine beneath the ground,
A funny treetop bond is found.
With laughter echoing through the air,
Nature's quirks make us all aware!

Secrets of the Silent Sentinels

Tall trees don't always stand so still,
They giggle with the gentle thrill.
A breeze will carry whispered laughs,
As branches shake like cheeky staffs.

The owls, with their knowledge vast,
Share giggles of the forest past.
They plot at dusk some silly schemes,
With echoes dancing through our dreams.

The shadows play a game of hide,
Each leaf a partner, side by side.
Who knew that silence could be fun?
As laughter mingles with the sun.

The winds confide in every knot,
In secrets shared, we find a spot.
Among the boughs, where shadows blend,
The humor in the heart will mend!

The Dance of the Drifting Leaves

The leaves decide to throw a ball,
With twirling steps, they rise and fall.
A rustling waltz, a spinning spree,
In colors bright for all to see.

The acorns strut in tiny suits,
While toadstools wear their best of boots.
With every gust, they leap and sway,
In joyful chaos, come what may.

And when the moon begins to rise,
The stars do wink with glimmered eyes.
Together they all spin and twirl,
In nature's earthen, leafy whirl.

As dawn approaches, leaves take flight,
In spirals, twisting with delight.
Their laughter mingles with the breeze,
In dance of life 'neath ancient trees!

The Wisdom of the Twisted Trails

In the woods, where paths do bend,
Raccoons argue, a playful trend.
They map the trails with their silly paws,
And declare the best way is full of flaws.

The squirrels debate on acorn's price,
While owls hoot, giving sage advice.
"Take the left, ignore the right!"
Then trip on roots, oh what a sight!

A bear rolls by, with glee and grace,
Chasing shadows at a frantic pace.
The trees just giggle, swaying in cheer,
As animals plot their mischief near.

So if you wander, heed this call,
The trails are funny, not wise at all.
Dance with your feet, let laughter prevail,
And follow the joy of a twisted trail.

Guardians of the Gnarled Grove

In a grove where the gnarled trees stand tall,
A clan of foxes hold the best brawl.
They guard their turf with jiggles and prance,
Inviting all critters to join the dance!

A wise old crow drops wisdom like seeds,
Saying, "Life's a circus, fulfilling our needs!"
The rabbits chuckle, as their ears flip,
While raccoons share snacks with a side of quips.

Hedgehogs roll in laughter, round and round,
Enjoying the chaos their pals have found.
"Who needs a throne? Just give us a log!"
They shout as they tease the pacing fog.

So if you meet the guardians here,
Join in the fun, hold nothing dear.
For life in the grove is laughter and cheer,
As nature's spirits dance, bringing all near.

Flickering Spirits of Fallen Leaves

Amid the leaves that twirl and dive,
Mischievous spirits come alive.
They flicker with laughter, giggles in air,
Playing peek-a-boo without a care.

The squirrels play tag, their tails all a-flutter,
While chattering loudly, causing a clutter.
"Catch me if you can!" one cries with glee,
And slips in the mud, oh what a spree!

The winds blow secrets through branches high,
As chipmunks chatter, passing them by.
A game of whispers, they try to decode,
"The nuts are running!" they burst and explode.

So watch for the flickers, don't miss the show,
Where laughter is plenty, and spirits will glow.
Join in the fun, let your worries cease,
And dance with the leaves, find your own peace.

The Heritage of High Branches

In the heights where the breezes flow,
Treetops whisper secrets, soft and slow.
Eagles crack jokes as they soar with flair,
While trees nod wisely, tousling their hair.

A family of owls play poker at night,
Counting their winks, what a sight!
The raccoons peek from a branch nearby,
Offering snacks with a twinkling eye.

Caterpillars tell tales of moths they'll be,
Belly-laughing over cups of tea.
And squirrels concoct plans for nutty gains,
Picturing heists with their tiny brains.

So embrace high branches, see the wise ways,
Join in the laughter, sing out your praise.
For in every whisper, there's joy to be found,
In the heritage of trees that surround.

Beneath the Boughs of Time

In the forest so wide, where the squirrels do play,
A acorn once whispered, 'Let's make a grand stay!'
But a wise old owl said, 'Now hold on my friend,
You'll just end up rolling, in leaves without end.'

The beavers were building, a lodge in the brook,
Chatted 'bout wisdom, they really could cook.
They made a fine dam, but it washed away quick,
They said, 'Next time let's use, some of that clever stick!'

The rabbits held meetings, in circles of grass,
Debating on lettuce, and which one would last.
But the wise old tortoise said, 'Don't worry at all,
Just plant some seeds, and you'll have a big haul!'

As the sun peeked through, the laughter ran free,
Nature's great lessons, brought joy, oh so glee.
With branches a-shaking, they danced round the pines,
In the realm of the creatures, where humor entwines.

Fireflies' Flashes of Insight

Once a firefly flickered, in a dark, moody night,
'Think glowing is easy? Oh, it's quite a plight!'
Another flashed back, 'But with just a short glow,
I can light up a dance, in the air to and fro.'

The crickets were chirping, with great wise intent,
Debating on rhythm, and what songs they'd invent.
'If we're off by a beat, the frogs will just jeer,'
One said with a laugh, 'Yet we still bring good cheer!'

A pair of bright beetles, donned hats made of leaves,
'We might not be wise, but let's not be deceived!
For style is a virtue, and confidence great,
Just roll with the buzz, and we'll dance 'til it's late!'

As the night rolled in, a party was born,
Beneath the tall trees, where no one felt worn.
With laughter and twinkles, they shined oh so bright,
In a world full of wisdom, they danced through the night.

The Spirit of the Sylvan

In a grove full of mushrooms, a gnome had a dream,
He thought he'd found wisdom, tucked under a beam.
But alas, it was only, a glow-worm's bright smile,
'Wisdom comes slowly, just rest for a while!'

A band of excited foxes played hide and seek,
They'd say, 'What's the secret? Let's give it a peek!'
The wise old raccoon said, 'It's simple my mates,
To be clever is great, but so are your fates!'

The trees whispered secrets, of ages gone by,
'The funniest lessons, come wrapped in a sigh.'
They chuckled and nodded, 'We're living our jest,
Get tangled in laughter and leave out the rest.'

As the evening fell, and the moon started peep,
The creatures of night painted dreams without sleep.
They danced in the shadows, with giggles and cheers,
For in their wise laughter, they conquered their fears.

Wisdom in the Wildflowers

A daisy once shouted, 'I know just the plan,
Let's form a big circle, and find out who can!'
The roses just giggled, 'Well, who really cares?
We're the prettiest flowers, it's all fun and flares!'

Buttercups chimed in, with a smirk on their bloom,
'I'll bet you can't guess, which flower has room!'
They all looked around, with their petals held wide,
And pondered about wisdom, while laughing with pride.

In the sun-drenched field, they swayed with the breeze,
The dandelions chuckled, 'We might spread with ease!'
But the violets piped up, 'It's not all about looks,
Wear your heart out loud, like the best little books!'

As twilight approached, the flowers shared rhymes,
Making merry with secrets, of nature's good times.
With laughter a-blooming, beneath the starry skies,
They found all their wisdom, in each other's wise eyes.

The Trail of the Timeless

On paths where squirrels bounce and play,
A wise old owl hoots night away.
Mice dance, their tiny feet don't tire,
While rabbits share tales by the fire.

The trees they giggle with every breeze,
Teaching us joy over worries with ease.
A chipmunk chimes in, insists on his jokes,
While the wise old fox winks at the folks.

Beneath the stars, in moon's silver glow,
We learn to laugh at the chaos we sow.
With each little step, we just take a chance,
In this silly grand nature's dance.

So gather your laughter, a capful or two,
Join in the fun; it's waiting for you.
With critters all chuckling, it's hard to complain,
On the trail of the timeless, we relish the gain.

Leafy Lessons of the Lark

A lark in the branches sings songs so spry,
While leaves whisper secrets, oh me, oh my!
'What's better than cheese?', asks a stout little worm,
The answer, of course, is a dance—take your turn!

The mushrooms all giggle, their caps popping high,
As they share wisdom from a nearby pie.
'Life is short,' says a snail, slowly, yet proud,
'Just measure your joy, not the size of the crowd!'

The sun spills laughter; the shadows all grin,
Every twig has a story; it's time to begin!
With camaraderie built on sweet nature's dough,
We learn from each other in the soil and the glow.

So gather 'round friends, let's share in the mirth,
In leafy lessons, we celebrate worth.
From the funny to silly, take every cue,
As we dance through the forest, there's always room for two!

Magpie's Melodies

A magpie chirps tunes that are cheeky and bright,
Gathering twigs for a nest just right.
With every odd treasure she finds, she will sway,
'These shiny things help me groove through the day!'

Her style is unique; there's glitter galore,
As she prances on branches, she's never a bore.
With a wink and a nod, she collects and she crafts,
Creating a symphony of giggles and drafts.

The trees listen close, nodding along,
As the magpie's sweet melodies mimic a song.
'Oh life is a stage, we are all in this play,
Just make sure your dance has some flair that can sway!'

So join in the chorus; let laughter resound,
As we share in the magic that's all around.
With melodies birthing a whimsical spree,
Our hearts take flight, wild and free!

A Tendency to Wander

In a forest where paths twist and turn,
A squirrel decides it's time for a yearn.
'Where to go now?' he scratches his head,
So off on an adventure, he joyfully sped.

With acorns in pockets and mischief galore,
He bumps into bushes, all filled with lore.
A hedgehog rolls by, grumbling with glee,
'This journey you're on looks just like me!'

Through puddles and prickers, they dance with delight,
Collecting odd stories that sparkle so bright.
They chat of the wonders there's no end in sight,
While butterflies laugh at their silly plight.

So wander, dear friends, on this trail of surprise,
With humor and joy as your daily prize.
You'll always discover that giggles abound,
In this world of mischief where true fun is found.

Rhythms of the Rustling Brush

In the whispers of leaves we dance and sway,
Squirrels giggle as they leap and play.
Mushrooms wear hats, colorful and bright,
Mice debate the best cheese for the night.

The branches above share juicy tales,
Of a raccoon who thinks he can sail.
He built a small boat from a fallen bark,
But ended up splashing—what a lark!

A wise old owl in a suit so fine,
Comments on fashion while sipping on brine.
He hoots for the critters to gather round,
To hear of the happenings in the ground.

So come join the fun in our rustling cheer,
Nature's a party, loud and clear.
With laughter and jokes, we'll tickle your mind,
In this giddy realm where joy's intertwined.

The Heart of the Hidden Hollow

In a nook of the trees, a party begins,
Frogs in tuxedos, all ready to spin.
With crickets on violins, they play a tune,
While fireflies flash like stars in June.

A hedgehog steps up, his dance quite bizarre,
He twirls and he whirls, it's a sight to spar.
The snails all groove with their shells shiny bright,
Each slip and slide is a comedic sight.

The badger in stripes brings forth the snacks,
While rabbits compare their acrobatic hacks.
With carrots and berries to munch and crunch,
They feast and they laugh at their silly hunch.

So if you peek into this hidden place,
You'll find creatures crafting a humorous space.
In the heart of the hollow, with giggles galore,
Join in the fun, who could ask for more?

Whispers of the Grove

In the shadows where mischief often hides,
The rabbits convene for some nonsensical rides.
With a wooden cart pulled by a bold little fox,
They race on the paths, dodging rocks in flocks.

A wise old tortoise makes puzzles of leaves,
While the chipmunks plot how to steal the peas.
A dance-off erupts with the squirrels in tow,
As the beret-wearing raccoon joins the show.

Beneath branches laughing, the fun never ends,
With tales of the drizzle where humor descends.
The trees move and creak, tickled by cheer,
As they share their secrets only critters can hear.

If laughter could echo through bark and through vine,
The stories of joy would be simply divine.
Join us in our grove where the smiles abound,
In the whispers and giggles where joy can be found.

Beneath the Canopy's Embrace

Underneath the sky, where the sun does peek,
A bear with a bowtie starts to speak.
He tells silly jokes about a fish who can fly,
While bees buzz with laughter, oh my how they try!

The owls hoot loudly, "Who's the wise one here?"
But it's a prancing deer who draws everyone near.
With antics so funny, he leaps and he bounds,
While the flowers giggle at the sights and sounds.

A raccoon in a beret serves pastries around,
But they're all just pinecones—smiles abound!
The porcupine juggles, with needles so spry,
He pricks at the curtain of clouds floating by.

So come dance in the sunlight, bring joy to your day,
Underneath the trees, where the creatures just play.
In the embrace of the green, where laughter's the best,
You'll find that the forest is truly a jest!

Secrets of the Ancient Trees

In the shade where squirrels play,
Old oaks whisper, 'Just eat hay!'
Their branches sway with giddy ease,
While mushrooms dance on wobbly knees.

Fungi giggle under bark,
Spying on the chattering lark.
They share gossip with the breeze,
'Did you hear about the bees?'

The Language of Leaves

Leaves rustle with tales untold,
'We've seen things both brave and bold!'
One leaf leans in, whispers 'Psst!',
'The dandelions think they're grand!'

Maples roll their eyes so wide,
'Oh dear, here comes the autumn ride!'
They sigh, but then the colors beam,
As if they've entered a dress-up dream.

Echoes of the Forest Floor

Underfoot, there's quite a show,
The critters chatter, 'Onward, go!'
A beetle boasts of daring feats,
'Oh please, just look at my fine seats!'

The moss chuckles at the ants,
'Did you see them do their dance?'
They stumble, juggle crumbs with flair,
While snails just smile and take their air.

Songs of the Sylvan Spirits

Spirits sing in playful tones,
Tickling rocks and ancient bones.
They make the shadows sway and waltz,
While teasing squirrels for their faults.

A raccoon winks, 'Join the fun!',
As twilight cradles the setting sun.
Together they leap, spin, and twirl,
In a forest-wide, magical whirl.

The Fox's Philosophies

In the shadows, sly and sleek,
The fox thinks thoughts so unique.
"Why chase a chicken, light on my feet?"
"When I can steal a feast, oh so sweet!"

With winks and grins, he prances about,
A riddle here, a riddle, no doubt.
"Why bark like a dog, when a wink will do?"
"In the world of wisdom, cheeky is true!"

Through whispering trees, he shares with the stag,
"Why be so serious? Just wave a flag!"
"Life's a banquet, not a dull chore,
So let's dance and play on the forest floor!"

With every laugh and clever scheme,
The fox spins stories, like a wild dream.
"In the glade of giggles, let spirits soar,
For wisdom's a laugh, and we all want more!"

Nature's Reverie

Beneath the boughs, the critters play,
They make mischief, come what may.
Squirrels chatter in leaps and bounds,
While ants dig tunnels undergrounds.

A bear slipped on a mossy stone,
With a huff and a grumble, he moans alone.
"Why is it slippery? Can't I just slide!"
As he tumbles down with ungraceful pride.

An owl hoots softly, wise and sage,
"Read a book? Nah, who needs that age!"
Finding fun in nocturnal flight,
"Just eat your snacks and be polite!"

In the ferny folds, the laughter roars,
As nature giggles and wisdom soars.
So when in doubt, just join the play,
For every creature has their own way!

The Hummingbird's Herald

A hummingbird zips, her wings a blur,
"I'm a news reporter, hear the sweet purr!"
"Did you see that bloom? It's quite the scene!"
"You'll want to taste nectar, it's fit for a queen!"

Her chatter buzzes, oh what a rush,
"The daffodils gossip, make quite the hush!"
"And don't you dare miss the dance of the bees,
For pollen is swirling, and they dance with ease!"

With a flash, she darts, spreading delight,
"In every petal, there's a story tonight!"
"Whisper to flowers, and they'll divine
A world full of magic, with nectar so fine!"

So gather round, all you flowers and trees,
For the tiny bird brings giggles with ease.
In a world of wonders, she'll spin you a yarn,
With each little hum, let your spirits be charmed!

Tranquility within Twisting Trails

On winding paths where shadows play,
The squirrels scamper, come what may.
"Why rush through life when you can meander?"
Squeaks one while hanging from the slander!

In tangled hedges, a rabbit frets,
"These leaves are a maze, I'm filled with regrets!"
"But in every twist, find some cheer,
For the carrot awaits just a hop from here!"

A turtle plods, with a wink and a shrug,
"Slow and steady? It's a warm snug!"
"Why race when the sun offers a glow?
Let's bask a while, let the worries go!"

So in the dappled light, where laughter swirls,
The creatures play through whirls and twirls.
Embrace the whimsy, shy not away,
In twisting trails, let fun lead the day!

www.ingramcontent.com/pod-product-compliance
Lightning Source LLC
Chambersburg PA
CBHW071854160426
43209CB00003B/547